REFLECTIONS
DURING THE WEEK
A Devotional

STEPHANIE LONG-SCOTT

CONTENTS

Preface 5
Acknowledgements 6
The Believer's Preamble 7
WEEK 1: Let God Use You 8
WEEK 2: Shine 10
WEEK 3: Obligation vs Opportunity 12
WEEK 4: Give Jesus the Service that He Paid for 14
WEEK 5: Details are Important 16
WEEK 6: God is Always Now 18
WEEK 7: God's Timing is Best 20
WEEK 8: God's Love is Not Earned 22
WEEK 9: You're Good Because God's Good 24
WEEK 10: The Valley of Dry Bones Starts With Us 26
WEEK 11: God's Storehouse Full of Good Things for You 28
WEEK 12: The Anointing of Unity 30
WEEK 13: Consider the Cost 32
WEEK 14: Respect Your Leadership 34
WEEK 15: You Never Know Who's Going to Run Into You 36
WEEK 16: The Heart of God in You 38
WEEK 17: Residue 40
WEEK 18: Controlled Burn 44
WEEK 19: God Prevents Us From Harm 46
WEEK 20: How We Should Present Ourselves to God ... 48
WEEK 21: God Requires Humility 50
WEEK 22: Listen to Jesus 52
WEEK 23: Stop, Look, Listen 54
WEEK 24: Little Faith, Big Miracle 56
WEEK 25: Bless Your Children 58
WEEK 26: A Kingdom Nation 60

WEEK 27: You are a Diamond	62
WEEK 28: You're Worthy to Receive Good from God	64
WEEK 29: The Power of God's Presence	66
WEEK 30: A Revelation about Isaiah 54:17	68
WEEK 31: Don't Own Sickness	70
WEEK 32: Who Had the Better Night's Sleep?	72
WEEK 33: Don't Prevent the Children from Coming to Jesus	74
WEEK 34: Well-Watered Trees	76
WEEK 35: God Will Not Forget You	78
WEEK 36: A Preponderance of the Evidence	80
WEEK 37: Your Family is Large	82
WEEK 38: God Speaks To Lions	84
WEEK 39: The Past is the Past	86
WEEK 40: Living Water	88
WEEK 41: Beautiful Feet	90
WEEK 42: A Love Never Seen Before	92
WEEK 43: Tomorrow About This Time	94
WEEK 44: Beware of the Company You Keep	96
WEEK 45: Cut the Umbilical Cord	98
WEEK 46: Break Through to Your Breakthrough	100
WEEK 47: Unsung Heroes	102
WEEK 48: Work With God to Get God Results	104
WEEK 49: I Know, But!	106
WEEK 50: From Thief to Evangelist	108
WEEK 51: O King, Live Forever!	110
WEEK 52: Love Forgave Us All	112
A Culmination of these 52 Weeks	114
A Prayer of Thanksgiving	116
The Road to Hell	118

All rights reserved. No part of this publication or its characters may be reproduced, distributed, or transmitted in any form or by any means, including photocopying, recording, or other electronic or mechanical methods, without the prior written permission of the publisher, except in the case of brief quotations embodied in reviews and certain other noncommercial uses permitted by copyright law.

©2025 Copyright Stephanie Long-Scott
All Rights Reserved.

Book Design: Lisa Monias
Printed in the United States of America

PREFACE

I realize that I cannot function unless I am being a blessing to someone: praying for them, helping them, giving to and encouraging them. This is who I am and I embrace it.

This weekly devotional is an expression of my heart for God and his people. It is full of real life examples that are relatable to everyone. There are "wisdom nuggets" to also chew on as you reflect each week on what the word of the Lord has said to you.

ACKNOWLEDGEMENTS

I would like to acknowledge the following people who contributed to the writing of this book:

Pastor Anthony Turkson, Rev. Janice Davis-Steele, Rev. Robin Smiley, Min. Jacqueline Carter, Rev. Reginald Johnson, Min. Tracy Dillard, Lady Robin Cooper, Min. Debra Duncan Heard, Min. Yvette Giles Thompson, Gina Hendrickson, and Min. Emmanuel Azu

This devotional is a collaborative work authored by Holy Spirit. Your spiritual insights brought revelation and elevation and I thank God for all of your lives.

Special shout out to Min. Jacqueline Carter and Min. Yvette Giles Thompson for your eagle eyes helping me proofread this work.

THE BELIEVER'S PREAMBLE

We the people of the Body of Christ

In order to form a more perfect union with Jesus

Establish truth

Insure peace

Provide for the common defense of the Gospel

Promote the general welfare of nations

Secure the blessings of liberty received from our Lord and Savior

In order to insure salvation for all

We do ordain and decree

This declaration of sovereignty to the Master of the universe

WEEK 1

Let God Use You

1 CORINTHIANS 3:9 - NKJV

For we are God's fellow workers; you are God's field, you are God's building.

One morning as I spoke with God I asked Him to allow me to be a light to someone.

I took my car to be serviced that day. While sitting in the lounge an elderly man came in. His hands and lips were trembling. I watched him for a few minutes. He didn't appear to be friendly or looked as if he wanted to be bothered. But the desire to please God overrode my apprehension to approach him.

I walked over sat next to him and said "Hello." I asked him if he believed in God. He said "Yes." I told him that I noticed his trembling and could I pray for him and he said "Yes." So I laid my hand on his and prayed. He was visibly appreciative. I smiled and returned to my seat.

This encounter is what I had asked God for. He enjoys displaying His love and compassion through us towards others.

God is going to present you with opportunities to bless someone this week. Be ready to work with God and to shine His light into someone's heart.

— S. Long-Scott

WISDOM NUGGET

The valiant keep it moving.
They will not be stuck in a place of complacency.

— REV. JANICE DAVIS-STEELE

WEEK 2

Shine

1 JOHN 4:17B • EPHESIANS 4:22-24 • EPHESIANS 5:1

We know from Psalms 104:2 that Jesus covers himself with light as with a garment. We also know that **1 John 4:17b** says … *as he is, so are we in this world.*

When you **PUT OFF** former conduct and are renewed in the spirit of your mind, you **PUT ON** the new You, created according to God, in true righteousness and holiness (**Ephesians 4:22-24**). Praise God, you have chosen the covering of Light. Jesus is the light of the world, so the light you have chosen or **PUT ON** is Christ (**Galatians 3:27**). Now, you are in the family of God, and are both poised and equipped to pierce the darkness through the light of the gospel of Christ.

As sons and daughters of the Most High God, our lives should reflect Jesus Christ, our LORD. We are to be imitators of him. Everywhere Jesus went, he was doing good. Everywhere we go, we take the true light of Jesus to that place. With love, grace, and compassion we represent Jesus. Those that have ears to hear will be able to SEE Jesus through us and come out of darkness into his marvelous light. In that light, they have eternal life.

You are God's vessel. So, go ahead, "Let your light so **shine** before men, that they may see your good works, and glorify your Father which is in heaven." (**Matthew 5:16 KJV**).

— Jaqueline Carter

WISDOM NUGGET

You Arise to Shine; to reflect the True Light, and take the gospel of Christ to the nations.

— Jacqueline Carter

WEEK 3

Obligation vs Opportunity

COLOSSIANS 3:23 - GNT

Whatever you do, work at it with all your heart, as though you were working for the Lord and not for people.

When you feel obligated to do something your heart generally isn't in it. You can't enjoy doing something out of a sense of duty or drudgery. But when you see it as an opportunity your whole perspective about what you're doing changes.

God gives us many opportunities to do well. He works His will in us and takes pleasure in doing so. **(Philippians 2:13)**.

So let's consider changing our "I got to" to "I get to" and our "I have to" to "I want to". It will relieve some of the stress we face in our daily lives. Apply this principle at work. Once your perspective changes you will become a better employee.

The same attitude adjustment works at home. What an outpouring of God's love everyone in your family can experience all because you seized the moment to be a blessing.

Let's ask ourselves this week if we really are the vessels that God can use. Let your answer be "Yes".

— S. Long-Scott

WISDOM NUGGET

True allegiance to God is when no one is watching and you're still doing things God's way.

— Stephanie Long-Scott

WEEK 4

Give Jesus the Service that He Paid for

A while ago I took my old car for A/C repair twice. But the problem wasn't fixed. Feeling frustrated as to what to do about it: whether to return to my mechanic or go somewhere else, I blurted out loud that I didn't have money to throw away. I want the service that I paid for! That became a "Selah" moment when I heard Holy Spirit say **"Jesus deserves the service that He paid for."**

Jesus was born to die so that I could live. His birth, death, and resurrection was His service to me. My acceptance of his gift of righteousness and living for Him is my service to Jesus.

I had to examine myself at that very moment regarding my attitude towards the Lord.

Romans 12:1 says for us to present ourselves as a living sacrifice holy and acceptable unto God which is our reasonable **service**. This is the foundation of our faith and love as members of the Body of Christ to avail ourselves to God.

Jesus' life must be as valuable to us as our lives are valuable to Him. It is God working through us both to will and to do of His good pleasure **(Philippians 2:13)** when we yield.

Let's reflect this week on how we can better serve the Lord and then allow the Lord to process us.

— S. Long-Scott

WISDOM NUGGET

When God does it and not you, then you are at rest.

— Pastor Anthony Turkson

WEEK 5

Details are Important

PROVERBS 14:12

There is a way that seems right to a man but its end is the way of death.

Sometimes we're not paying attention to the instructions we're given because we're doing them by rote not realizing that the details can change.

Moses was instructed to strike the rock the first time and water came out **(Exodus 17:6)**. But he was told to speak to the rock the second time **(Numbers 20:8, 11)**. Moses didn't pay attention and struck the rock.

I imagined Moses saying to himself, "Water out of the rock; oh yes I'll just strike it like before." Wrong! Moses wasn't allowed to enter into the Promised Land for his failure to adhere to the details.

Pay attention to what God tells you. He may have told you to do something a certain way several times before but the next time the details may change.

Be ready to flow with God this week **without assumption**.

— S. Long-Scott

WISDOM NUGGET

Even under grace obedience is required.

— Anthony Turkson

WEEK 6

God is Always Now

Do you realize that God is now right now? He's an ever present help in times of trouble **(Psalm 46:1)**.

God created the time and space continuum but He is not bound by it. He is eternal and moves in and out of time.

Keep God current by speaking about Him in the now. **He is I AM (Exodus 3:14)**.

Bring the **now** into play by saying things that agree with God being **now**:

- I am healed now.
- I am prospering now.
- My whole house is blessed now.
- I am overcoming every trial now.
- My gifts are making room for me now.
- I am being promoted now.
- I am fulfilling God's purpose in my life now.

This is your faith speaking **(2 Corinthians 4:13)**. God will manifest what you believe right now so don't grow weary.

Speak Now this week!".

— S. Long-Scott

WISDOM NUGGET

When you're disciplined, you will do what others won't.
You will have what others can't.

— Rev. Janice Davis-Steele

WEEK 7

God's Timing is Best

PROVERBS 15:23 (THE PASSION TRANSLATION)

Everyone enjoys giving great advice.
But how delightful it is to say the right thing at the right time!

I wanted to encourage a dear friend but God wouldn't let me. I had to wait for his timing. He knew that my friend wasn't ready to hear what I wanted to say even though the words were seasoned with salt. God had to prepare their heart first. When God gave me permission to speak, my words were easily received.

"So then, my beloved brethren, let every man be swift to hear, slow to speak, slow to wrath" **(James 1:19)**.

Though our intentions can be good to say or do something, we still need to wait on God to know when to execute.

We will have several encounters in the course of this week to apply these scriptures in our discussions. Stay tuned into God's promptings.

— S. Long-Scott

WISDOM NUGGET

Don't speak out of turn.
— Stephanie Long-Scott

WEEK 8

God's Love is Not Earned

1 JOHN 4:8-11 NKJV

He who does not love does not know God, for God is love. In this the love of God was manifested toward us, that God has sent His only begotten Son into the world, that we might live through Him. In this is love, not that we loved God, but that He loved us and sent His Son to be the propitiation for our sins. Beloved, if God so loved us, we also ought to love one another.

While babysitting my granddaughter, she became a little rambunctious so I gave her a stern look. Thinking that I was angry with her she ran up to me hugging and kissing me excessively.

I shared this account with my daughter-in-law telling her that this was a tactic my granddaughter was using to get her way. But my daughter-in-law told me that it was my granddaughter's defense mechanism to get me to not withhold my love from her. I got a confirmation in my spirit.

It brought tears to my eyes reflecting on the anxiety that my granddaughter must have experienced in that moment. I don't want her to EVER feel she has to go through gyrations in order to get me to love her.

God doesn't require us to do anything for Him to love us. He just does.

Let's take spiritual inventory this week to make sure that we are not using love as blackmail.

— S. Long-Scott

WISDOM NUGGET

Let your love be like breathing.
— STEPHANIE LONG-SCOTT

WEEK 9

You're Good Because God's Good

GENESIS 1:31A - KJV

And God saw every thing that he had made, and behold, it was very good.

God cannot lie. Whatever good I see in my life is because of God who Himself is good.

James 1:17 says every good and perfect gift is from above and comes down from the Father of lights who doesn't change. He wasn't going to allow the devil to mess up his good and perfect creation so he sent Jesus to restore us by taking out of us that which was not good and perfect: **the sin nature**.

Receiving Jesus restores our spirits to perfection because the Holy Spirit comes inside of us to dwell. And where the spirit of the Lord is, there is liberty (**2 Corinthians 3:17**).

So say this to yourself this week:

I come from Good and Perfect. Made in the image of Good and Perfect. That makes me good and perfect spiritually.

— S. Long-Scott

WISDOM NUGGET

Righteousness is a gift.
When worn it changes your state of being.

— Stephanie Long-Scott

WEEK 10

The Valley of Dry Bones Starts With Us

SCRIPTURE REFERENCE: EZEKIEL 37: 1-14

Do you have a question you have asked God on more than one occasion? I have and it is, "God, what can I do to help get the word out about You and Your Kingdom?" Scripture is always the best place for a fresh revelation. While studying the first fourteen verses of **Ezekiel 37**, the Holy Spirit stirred me in response.

God has already placed us where we can make a powerful impact. It is our immediate sphere of influence, our homes, families, jobs, and places we frequent just by living out our daily lives. We must be willing to walk where he is leading us with eyes open and a willingness to serve where we have already been placed. It is sad to think or even know that not everyone is alive in Christ. The Walking Dead is someone walking outside of a life with knowing Jesus. Like Ezekiel we must know with confidence and hope that God can resuscitate any dead thing **(verses 1-3)**.

We must be a willing conduit to work in our valley. God told Ezekiel to prophesy over the bones. To prophesy is to speak God's word to the people of our own time, calling them to a covenant relationship of faithfulness. We must proclaim God's word with abundant confidence. We must be willing to testify how we too were once among the valley of dry bones until the day we accepted that only Jesus could make us alive and whole **(verses 4-6)**.

We must also be willing to boldly pray for the spirit to move in the power of faith. Then we must submit to the work of the Holy Spirit and allow the spirit to do the rest. Understanding the work of the Holy Spirit is essential and will position us for the next step. We must be prepared to do what is necessary for dry bones to become a people revived into an army of service. Everyone has gifts and talents that can be used to pour into others as the kingdom of God is continually being added to **(verses 7-10)**.

I love when God reveals the 'why' to the questions I ask of Him. When He brings into my remembrance why I am equipped for the valley assignment. I can remember how I felt; dried up, lost, and I lived a life without hope. You see someone walked through the valley of dried bones for me. I am so grateful Jesus revived me from the dead, embodied me with God's spirit, and I can fully live in Christ **(verses 11-14)**.

We must always stay connected to Christ and not lose hope by focusing on the things we see in the world we live in. We must look where He directs us and be available to move where He leads. There is always work to do but are we prepared to go where He sends us, talk to whom he puts in our path, and to boldly continue the work of revival in the valley of dry bones.

— Tracy Dillard

WISDOM NUGGET

Commit to the commission of souls.

— Stephanie Long-Scott

WEEK 11

God's Storehouse Full of Good Things for You

PSALMS 16:5-6 COMPLETE JEWISH BIBLE

Adonai, my assigned portion, my cup: you safeguard my share. Pleasant places were measured out for me; I am content with my heritage.

This is good news. What God has for you is for YOU. No need to covet someone else's possessions. No need to be envious of others. The Bible says the earth is the Lord's and the fullness thereof (**Psalm 24:1**); so everything belongs to God anyway.

God doesn't need to take from someone else to give to you. There's enough provision in God's storehouse with your name on it.

Consider creating a "My Gratitude to God List". Holy Spirit will reveal to you all that God has already provided. Go over your list again and again. You will begin to have an attitude of gratitude causing God to give you even more.

What's yours is yours alone.

— S. Long-Scott

WISDOM NUGGET

Reclaim your focus: there are new opportunities ahead.

— Rev. Janice Davis-Steele

WEEK 12

The Anointing of Unity

PSALMS 133:1-2

Behold, how good and how pleasant it is for brethren to dwell together in unity! It is like the precious oil upon the head, running down on the beard, the beard of Aaron, running down on the edge of his garments.

God comes to anoint us when we are unified. This unity is based on God's love for us and His desire to be with us and to dwell in us:

ACTS 2:1-4 - NKJV

When the Day Pentecost had fully come, they were all with one accord in one place. And suddenly there came a sound from heaven, as of a rushing mighty wind, and it filled the whole house where they were sitting. Then there appeared to them divided tongues, as of fire, and one sat upon each of them. And they were all filled with Holy Spirit and began to speak with other tongues, as the Spirit gave them utterance.

"And they were all filled with Holy Spirit"; filled with God's glory; filled with the ability to communicate with Holy Spirit; filled with holy fire to burn up the chaff of the enemy within and without. This is God's desire **(2 Corinthians 6:16)**.

We are the Body of Christ; God's house. And a house divided cannot stand **(Matthew 12:25)**. The devil is no match against us when we stand as one man in Christ. He knows that we are a force to be reckoned with but do we?

Holy Spirit show us where we may have hindered you from flowing freely in our lives. Remind us that we are united in your love Lord God.

— S. Long-Scott

WISDOM NUGGET

The glory of God is God throwing his weight around.

— Pastor Anthony Turkson

WEEK 13

Consider the Cost

LUKE 14:28, 33 (TPT)

So don't follow me without considering what it will cost you. For who would construct a house before first sitting down to estimate the cost to complete it? Likewise, unless you surrender all to me, giving up all you possess, you cannot be one of my disciples.

It's one thing to follow someone for the benefits they bring, and completely another when you're asked to be like that person.

Those of us that have made Jesus the Lord of our lives are required to pattern our lives after Him. This is no small feat but God's grace is sufficient to help us **(2 Corinthians 12:9)**. Jesus told us that we would experience trials and tribulations but to be of good cheer because He has overcome the world on our behalf.

In **Luke 9:23** Jesus tells us that in order to follow Him we must deny ourselves and take up our cross daily. The cross we're asked to bear doesn't compare to the weight of the cross Jesus carried. He carried the weight of the world upon his shoulder.

We don't come up short walking with Jesus because He is a rewarder to them that diligently seek Him **(Hebrews 11:6)**.

Reflect this week on this: How much dying are you willing to do in order to live the life that Jesus died for you to have?

— S. Long-Scott

WISDOM NUGGET

Christ gives us the strength to endure and enables us to reign with him.

— Jacqueline Carter

WEEK 14

Respect Your Leadership

HEBREWS 13:7,17 (NKJV)

Remember those who rule over you, who have spoken the word of God to you, whose faith follow, considering the outcome of their conduct. Obey those who rule over you, and be submissive, for they watch out for your souls, as those who must give account. Let them do so with joy and not with grief, for that would be unprofitable for you.

Respect must be given to our spiritual leaders. Whoever God has placed you under, follow them as they follow Christ **(1 Corinthians 11:1)**. Pray for them. Thank God for them. Speak well words into their lives. Bless them financially. They bear us up before the Lord in prayer which is a huge responsibility. They've taught us the word of God. They've taught us how to pray. They've taught us how to be leaders. They've taught us how to believe God for ourselves.

Instead of running to them with grievances, give them a praise report. Testify of the goodness of God. Let's show them how we've applied the word in our lives.

Don't let your pastors grow weary in well doing **(Galatians 6:9)**. But thank them for their leadership and a job well done.

This week ask God how you can specifically express His love to your pastor.

— S. Long-Scott

WISDOM NUGGET

A weak Gospel is not going to feed a strong Christian.

— Rev. Robin Smiley

WEEK 15

You Never Know Who's Going to Run Into You

COLOSSIANS 4:5-6 – NLT

Live wisely among those who are not believers, and make the most of every opportunity. Let your conversation be gracious and attractive so that you will have the right response for everyone.

I was rear ended once as I came to a stop at an intersection. I looked in my rear view mirror and saw the guy who bumped me getting out of his truck. I kept my composure, put on my flashers and got out of my car. I checked for damage but there was none.

I asked the guy if he was on his phone and he said no. He admitted that he had looked away for only a second. He explained that his sister was on his mind. She was hospitalized and he was on his way to see her. His sister had terminal cancer and he wanted her saved before she died.

While he was speaking I took his hands and agreed with him in prayer for his sister's healing and salvation. There we were standing in the street while the traffic continued by.

He then said that he didn't know why he had driven in this particular direction to the hospital. I told him for no other reason but for him to *run into me* so that I could pray for him.

Saints we never know when or where God's going to use us but be ready this week and be bold.

— S. Long-Scott

WISDOM NUGGET

We yield. He fills.

— Stephanie Long-Scott

WEEK 16

The Heart of God in You

MATTHEW 9:36 (TPT)

When he saw the vast crowds of people, Jesus' heart was deeply moved with compassion, because they seemed weary and helpless, like wandering sheep without a shepherd.

While employed at a utility company I did a lot of volunteer work. During Discount Utility Day thousands of people would come to get help with their utility bills. As an intake person I filled out forms with the ID's and bills that the people presented to me. Desperate people looking for someone to listen to them and to understand. Many falling on hard times through no fault of their own.

On this particular day 7,000 people had been processed. Though I'd been there for 12 hours I felt good because I had had the opportunity to pray for many of them.

On my way home on the metro a spirit of heaviness overwhelmed me. When I got off the train and into my car the burden was still there. Arriving home I asked God what was wrong with me. He told me that I had carried 7,000 people home in my heart and to pray for them. I literally fell to my knees weeping and praying. It was only when the burden lifted out of my spirit that I was able to rise. That was the first time I ever experienced true empathy.

We who are the salt and light in this dark world must shine forth allowing God to use us.

When God places people on your heart this week please pray. You will be saving a life.

— S. Long-Scott

WISDOM NUGGET

You may know the books of the Bible but do you know the voice of God.

— Rev. Robin Smiley

WEEK 17

Residue

Residue: something that remains after a part is removed; disposed of or used; remainder; rest; remnant

Synonyms: debris, garbage, junk, scraps, scum, leftovers

How many of you know that God doesn't want us to hurt? If something is gnawing at us He will help us to remove it. But the first thing is to recognize that it is there. It's not easy facing truths about ourselves but that is half of the healing process.

I was expecting a sizable financial blessing some time ago along with some other folks. I was so excited. I am a giver and have sown into so many ministries and other worthy causes. I told myself that this was my harvest getting ready to manifest. It was my turn to be financially blessed. I felt that I deserved it. I had prayed several prayers of agreement with others who were expecting this financial windfall. I began doing an action prophecy by getting rid of old things in anticipation of the new things coming. I remained excited right up until I got the news that I was not a recipient of the blessing. Everyone that I had prayed for received good news. I was stunned. How could this be? Why was I passed over? What had I done to deserve this slight? I was genuinely happy for everyone else and said so. But deep inside, I was hurt.

Initially, I needed an attitude adjustment. You can only get that by being in the presence of the Lord. If you can't be honest with God you're in trouble. I did most of the talking that day. I made sure that I had forgiven those who thought I was not a candidate for this financial blessing and those who didn't fight for me to get it. God asked me would I rather put Him in a box or allow Him freedom to bless me anyway He saw fit. Of course

I responded "No". Put God in a financial box? That would be crazy on my part. I felt better after talking to God. So I went on with my life.

Over the years, every time the incident came up whether I spoke to someone who had benefited from the financial blessing or someone asked me about what happened, I would feel this hurt deep inside of me rise up. Though it didn't linger long, it was still there. These were opportunities God was giving me to confront this pain but I ignored them and kept moving forward physically but not emotionally. What I had done was put myself inside a box of hurt without realizing it. This pain was the residue of the incident from years ago. But the Holy Spirit is so gentle and kind and didn't want me to hurt any longer. He wasn't going to allow that residue to remain in me.

Just recently I called someone to encouragement them about something they had said publicly. I wanted them to know that I completely understood what they had said and thanked them for their boldness to speak. Well out of nowhere I admitted that I was still hurt from this past incident and I actually used the word residue. It was like the Holy Spirit blindsided me and made me speak about this latent pain outwardly to someone else. The bible says that we should confess our faults one to another for healing (James 5:16). I couldn't believe how liberated I felt after speaking aloud. I was free of that residue in an instant. God is so amazing.

What God spoke to me in that moment was that I should be more excited than ever before about Him blessing me financially. The blessings are coming in God's timing and he wants me poised to receive. That residue was blocking the financial flow that the Lord wanted to bring me. But now, Hallelujah, Lord have your way! You are the same yesterday, TODAY, and forever (Hebrews 13:8). I run with his financial promises to me. I open up my heart and mind to receive 7-8 figure financial increase. The limits are off.

My situation here was financial. But this can apply to other aspects of life. Pain is pain. It is an emotion which we must come face to face with or we'll never be free of it. You can lock away pain instead of getting rid of it. When you lock it up, you're in a mode of self-protection. It is like a closet you never go into but you throw stuff in and closed the door telling yourself you will deal with the contents later. But you don't.

I leave you with this: Open that closet door and let the contents fall out. It's time to take emotional inventory so that God can bring what he wants you to have in life. Take off the limits you place on God to bless you. Don't box yourself in with a negative mindset. Exchange his blessings for the trash you've been holding onto and actually protecting. Like Mary in Luke 1:38 accept what the Lord says about you and agree with him by saying "Be it unto me according to thy word". Let the Lord continue to be magnified and manifested. Amen.

WISDOM NUGGET

Don't use pain as your ink when you're writing your life story.

— Rev Janice Davis-Steel

WEEK 18

Controlled Burn

HEBREWS 12:28-29 (NKJV)

Wherefore we receiving a kingdom which cannot be moved, let us have grace, whereby we may serve God acceptably with reverence and godly fear: For our God is a consuming fire.

Controlled burn involves setting planned fires to maintain the health of the forest; often to prepare the area for new vegetation.

God showed me the Body of Christ as a spiritual forest, and He was setting mini fires throughout. **Isaiah 61:3** mentions believers as trees of righteousness, the planting of the Lord. **Psalm 92:12** says the righteous shall flourish like a palm tree and grow like a cedar in Lebanon.

When God's garden (The Body of Christ) starts to accumulate a lot of weeds and overgrowth, the Lord has to burn it away **(Psalms 97:3)**. His holy fire doesn't harm us but helps us. Our trees will not be consumed because of the purifying blood of Jesus that makes us holy.

So if you feel some heat this week it is the Lord at work clearing out the clutter in His forest. He will not allow anything to stunt your growth; not even you!

— S. Long-Scott

WISDOM NUGGET

God creates the fire. He controls the heat.

— Stephanie Long-Scott

WEEK 19

God Prevents Us From Harm

DANIEL 6:21-22

Then Daniel said to the king, O king, live forever: My God sent His angel and shut the lions' mouths, so that they have not hurt me, because I was found innocent before Him;

As God saved Daniel from the lions, he saved me from a pack of dogs.

I left my house on my way to work one morning with car keys in hand. As I approached my car I saw three dogs running fast towards me. I made it to my car but not in time to open the door and get in. The dogs stopped about five feet away from me growling and barking. I would not look at them. I heard Holy Spirit say "Show no fear". I took a deep breath. Then I turned my head with my face set like flint looking at them intently and said "IN THE NAME OF JESUS" (**Philippians 2:10**). They turned and ran away.

I tried to put my car key into the car door but to no success because I was shaking so much. The adrenaline rush finally passed.

I never saw those dogs again. I believe they may have seen one of my angels (**Psalms 91:11**). But I know of a surety that God had intervened on my behalf.

This week acknowledge God's presence in your life; His ability to love, protect, and defend you from all hurt, harm, and danger. And thank Him from a grateful heart.

— S. Long-Scott

WISDOM NUGGET

Don't change your position just let God remove the mountain before you.

— Yvette Giles Thompson

WEEK 20

How We Should Present Ourselves to God

PSALM 15 (NLT)

Who may worship in your sanctuary, Lord?
Who may enter your presence on your holy hill?

Those who lead blameless lives and do what is right,
speaking the truth from sincere hearts.

Those who refuse to gossip or harm their neighbors or speak evil of their friends.

Those who despise flagrant sinners, and honor the faithful followers
of the Lord, and keep their promises even when it hurts.

Those who lend money without charging interest,
and who cannot be bribed to lie about the innocent.

Such people will stand forever.

Let this Psalm be your meditation this week.

— S. Long-Scott

WISDOM NUGGET

Without God we cannot be like God.

— Emmanuel Azu

WEEK 21

God Requires Humility

PROVERBS 18:12 TPT

A man's heart is the proudest when his downfall is nearest, for he won't see glory until the Lord sees humility.

King Nebuchadnezzar learned the hard way the consequences of being prideful **(Daniel 4:24-25)**. It took him seven years living like an animal before he acknowledged that God was the Most High.

James 4:6 says that God resists the proud but gives grace to the humble. Since the spirit of pride is not of God, He cannot use it to bring His blessings to us.

This is not the time to be resisting the promptings of God to change our behavior. More turbulent times are coming and no one will be exempt.

We all will have to account for the decisions we make in this life **(Romans 14:11-12)**. Let's make sure we're on the Lord's side when that time comes.

Read Daniel Chapter 4 this week. Then ask yourself if you need a change of heart.

— S. Long-Scott

WISDOM NUGGET

Your exaltation is measured by your humility.

— Stephanie Long-Scott

WEEK 22

Listen to Jesus

JOHN 2:3-5; 11 - NKJV

And when they ran out of wine, the mother of Jesus said to Him, "They have no wine." Jesus said to her, "Woman, what does your concern have to do with Me? My hour has not yet come." His mother said to the servants, **"Whatever He says to you, do it."** *This beginning of signs Jesus did in Cana of Galilee, and manifested His glory; and His disciples believed in Him.*

This is Jesus' first recorded miracle, turning water into wine. We see Mary, the mother of Jesus yielding to Jesus' spiritual authority. Mary was human just like us. Jesus was God manifested in human flesh.

So to those whose religious beliefs places Mary above Jesus, hear what Mary says to all of us, **"Whatever He (Jesus) says to you, do it."**

Jesus instructs that if we ask anything in his name he would do it **(John 14:14)**. Remember no one else has the power to save us from sin except Jesus.

This week reflect on how you are praying. Prayers prevented from reaching heaven are prayers that have not been directed there. If we really are the vessels that God can use, let your answer be "Yes."

— S. Long-Scott

WISDOM NUGGET

If you pray to the saints you are praying to yourselves.

— Pastor Anthony Turkson

WEEK 23

Stop, Look, Listen

PSALM 32:8 - NKJV

I will instruct you and teach you in the way you should go;
I will guide you with My eye.

This scripture says that God is watching us even though we might not want him involved in our lives. He is ready to counsel us if we are willing.

To those of us that want God involved, he has the right to tell us which way to go. We must listen to God with every step we take. It's like you're walking along with God and he says "Stop, look, and listen." Hear what God says and shows you before you proceed.

We all have come to crossroads in life not knowing which path to take. But God tells us in **Psalm 119:105** that his word is a lamp to our feet and a light to our path.

We won't ever go wrong following him. This should be our daily interaction with God.

Reflect this week on the way your life has been going. Have you really been listening to His voice or your own?

— S. Long-Scott

WISDOM NUGGET

Either you can take the example or you can be the example.

— Deborah Duncan Heard

WEEK 24

Little Faith, Big Miracle

MATTHEW 14:26-31

And when the disciples saw him walking on the sea, they were troubled, saying, It is a spirit; and they cried out for fear. But straightway Jesus spake unto them, saying, Be of good cheer; it is I; be not afraid. And Peter answered him and said, Lord, if it be thou, bid me come unto thee on the water. And he said, Come. **And when Peter was come down out of the ship, he walked on the water**, *to go to Jesus. But when he saw the wind boisterous, he was afraid; and beginning to sink, he cried, saying, Lord, save me. And immediately Jesus stretched forth his hand, and caught him, and said unto him, O thou of little faith, wherefore didst thou doubt?*

Peter walked on water. Other than Jesus, he is the only human being to do so. Yes, he got distracted looking at the wind. But don't concentrate on that. Peter **WALKED ON WATER**. When Peter walked on water he was also walked on the Word of God **(Ephesians 5:26)**. Also note that Peter had to walk back to the boat **with Jesus** while the storm was still raging. It is only when they both had climb into the boat that the storm ceased **(Matthew 14:32)**.

Little faith doesn't mean no faith. Little faith can still accomplish great things.

Be encouraged and don't allow the devil to convince you that you don't have faith in God.

Reflect on what your faith in God has already accomplished in your life and continue to believe God for more.

— S. Long-Scott

WISDOM NUGGET

You know you believe when you show you believe.

— Rev. Janice Davis-Steele

WEEK 25

Bless Your Children

3 JOHN 1:4 – NKJV

I have no greater joy than to hear that my children walk in truth.

———

Every opportunity I get to be with my granddaughter, I speak into her life. I started a tradition that any time I get to watch her we begin our day with prayer. I make sure she hears me tell her that she's a world changer, intelligent, successful and a kingdom builder. She knows she's loved. I still speak into the life of my son and daughter-in-law. Please don't pass up the opportunity to bless your children.

Here are just a few scriptures to speak over them:

Ephesians 2:10 - You were created for a purpose.

Jeremiah 29:11 - God has a plan for your life.

Psalm 139:14 - You are uniquely made.

Psalm 127:3 - You are a gift from God.

1 Corinthians 13:8 - God's love for you will never fail.

Set a precedent for your children and grandchildren that the succeeding generations can build upon. If you haven't you can start today.

— S. Long-Scott

WISDOM NUGGET

The privilege is yours but the power is His.

— Rev. Janice Davis-Steele

WEEK 26

A Kingdom Nation

1 PETER 2:9 – NKJV

But you are a chosen generation, a royal priesthood, a holy nation, His own special people, that you may proclaim the praises of Him who called you out of darkness into His marvelous light;

Every believer in the shed blood of Jesus Christ for salvation is now a member of this holy nation. This means that you now have dual citizenship: the county where you were born naturally and your heavenly citizenship **(Philippians 3:20)**.

This holy nation transcends all other nations because it is not based on race, color, or natural origins. **It is a spirit nation.** King Jesus our Sovereign Ruler, rules from heaven; a kingdom that has no end. He rules in the heart of every believer. He has delegated His kingdom authority and power to his Body here on earth. Every member of his Body must walk in and be controlled by the Spirit. This means we see each other beyond this 3D flesh realm **(2 Corinthians 5:16)**.

Let's not allow the devil to use our skin color to divide us. He has no business in our affairs.

Let's really reflect on this revelation. Try to describe someone you know without using race or any accent they may have. Like Dr. Martin Luther King, describe them by the content of their character. You'll be amazed how well you know them.

— S. Long-Scott

WISDOM NUGGET

We are most challenged in the area that we are most powerful.

— Stephanie Long-Scott

WEEK 27

You are a Diamond

No matter how much dirt you throw on a diamond when you wash it off it's still a diamond. God's people are diamonds and His word is the water that keeps them clean **(Ephesians 5:26 NKJV)**.

There are many facets to a diamond and it glows with the glory of God. **(2 Corinthians 3:18 NKJV)**.

Diamonds have sharp edges in their natural state. This is evidence of its purity **(John 15:3 NLT)**.

A diamond is resistant to being scratched except by another diamond **(Ephesians 4:29-32 NKJV)**.

Ezekiel 3:8-9 CSB says God has made us like a diamond which is harder than flint. In this world where people are easily offended we must have a tough exterior. We have the ability to withstand and oppose our enemy.

We cannot minister the Gospel of Jesus Christ in a weakened condition. We must continue to let the word of God keep us clean, fortified, and shining like never before.

Reflect on your strength in the Lord this week and know that you are able to withstand any attack from the enemy. Be the resilient person that God has created you to be. We really are the vessels that God can use.

— S. Long-Scott

WISDOM NUGGET

You don't have to be a slave to other people's opinions.

— Janice Davis-Steele

WEEK 28

You're Worthy to Receive Good from God

PSALM 84:11 (TPT)

For the Lord is brighter than the brilliance of a sunrise! Wrapping himself around me like a shield, he is so generous with his gifts of grace and glory. Those who walk along his paths with integrity will never lack one thing they need, for he provides it all!

My 15yr old car had been getting a lot of repairs of late but I didn't want to part with it. She finally broke down and needed to be towed. I informed my son and gave him the name of the dealership I was headed to. He texted me a picture of a car at the dealership telling me to at least explore the possibility of getting a new car. I really wasn't interested but decided to inquire.

I showed the salesman the picture of the car and he insisted it wasn't there. He had never seen it before. I gave him the stock number which he verified and went looking for it. 15 minutes later he pulled up in the car. He told me he found it in the back of the dealership. None of the other salesmen had seen the car before either. **It was hidden away for me!**

I heard Holy Spirit say that I was worthy of something new and to stop selling myself short. This was a pivot point to think differently about myself.

God has been showing you his will for your life. Open your heart and mind to receive the gifts that God wants to bring specifically to you. You matter to God.

— S. Long-Scott

WISDOM NUGGET

Don't believe everything you think.
What you think sometimes may be wrong.

— Pastor Anthony Turkson

WEEK 29

The Power of God's Presence

PSALM 97:3, 5 (NKJV)

A fire goes before Him, And burns up His enemies round about. The mountains melt like wax at the presence of the Lord, at the presence of the Lord of the whole earth.

The same God whose presence can melt a mountain can bring peace, comfort, and refreshment. The same God who can cause the earth to tremble and dry up the seas is our place of refuge and strength.

I had an open vision of a dear friend in Christ standing before the Lord but there was also a mountain in front of her. The mountain melted and my friend was told to enter into the presence of the Lord.

I heard the Lord say:

"It all depends on who is standing before Me what the result of being in My presence will be."

Acknowledge God's presence with you wherever you find yourself this week. He will meet you in the kitchen while cooking; or as you take a shower (something about the water makes it easy to hear his voice); or while you are driving.

Wherever you are He is there **(Matthew 1:23b)**.

— S. Long-Scott

WISDOM NUGGET

The seal of the Holy Spirit has made us tamper proof.

— Emmanuel Azu

WEEK 30

Who do you turn to when you cast your cares?

1 PETER 5:7(NLT)

Give all your worries and cares to God, for he cares about you.

We cast our cares to God, not the world. Knowing our disposition in the wait will keep us grounded in his Word.

Live your life free from the love of money and be content because He will never leave you or forsake you **(Hebrews 13:5)**. Humble yourself before the Lord so that He will show you favor and give you more grace to endure any circumstance. **(James 4:6; Proverbs 3:35)** Live a Godly life, free of wrongdoing because you know as a joint heir with Christ Jesus, you will inherit the Kingdom of God. **(1 Corinthians 6:9; Isaiah 1:16)**. "I have already supplied your every need, and you lack nothing", says the Lord. Be content in all that you have in all circumstances **(Philippians 4:11)** and be reminded that all you have belongs to God. Have the patience to endure as God has and will always be patient with you. He is never slow in keeping His promise to you **(2 Peter 3:9)**. His Word says that he will exalt you because you have humbled yourself and he will lift you up **(Matthew 23:12; James 4:10)**. Work his Word as tools in your body, mind and spirit.

This week let us focus on the joy that has been set before us, JESUS.

— Gina Hendrickson

WISDOM NUGGET

Comparison can cause you to doubt who you are in Christ Jesus.

— Gina Hendrickson

WEEK 31

Don't Own Sickness

ROMANS 3:3-4 - KJV

For what if some did not believe? Shall their unbelief make the faith of God without effect?
*God forbid: yea, **let God be true, but every man a liar;** as it is written,*

The devil wants us to focus on facts instead of the word of God which is the truth. His modus operandi is to stop us from believing God through fear.

Going through a sickness or a financial trial is challenging enough. But when the heat is turned up it can cause anyone to doubt. But God tells us to fear not only believe **(Mark 5:36)**.

Don't possess sickness by saying "My arthritis, my cancer, etc." It's an invitation from the devil to take ownership. So refuse the invitation. Instead take the healing scriptures and declare the decree of healing over yourself.

If you repeat healing scriptures over and over and out loud to yourself you will eventually believe what you are saying. And your body will begin to respond to the truth (Isaiah 53:5, 1 Peter 2:24).

I suffered allergies growing up: dust, grass, trees, and furry animals. I was miserable. When I became an adult I developed nasal polyps. My taste and smell disappeared. I had surgery in 1988. The ENT doctor said that they would probably return. I didn't know Jesus then. In 1990 the polyps returned. This was the year that I made Jesus the Lord of my life.

I went back to the same doctor. He asked me when I wanted to schedule surgery. I never went back after that. I took Isaiah 53:5 as my medicine. I was a babe in Christ so this was the only scripture that I knew for healing. I wore this scripture out. I declared it every day and night for months.

One day while I was cooking I got a whiff of the food and then it was gone. Immediately the devil told me that I hadn't smelled anything. But I shut down his words in my mind and said out loud that I did smell the food. It took another three weeks before my smell and taste returned. Glory to God!

It was 26 years later that I had to see another ENT doctor. Upon his examination he marveled at the skill of the surgeon that had removed the polyps. I told him it was Dr. Jesus but he acted like he didn't hear me. But it didn't matter because I know who touched me and healed me.

This week reflect on how you speak over yourself. Though we tend to think only of physical sickness there is also emotional illness, financial illness and such that need healing.

Choose to speak life only **(John 6:63)**.

— S. Long-Scott

WISDOM NUGGET

I declare sickness a symptom.

— Lady Robin Cooper

WEEK 32

Who Had the Better Night's Sleep?

DANIEL 6:18 NIV

"Then the king returned to his palace and spent the night without eating and without any entertainment being brought to him. And he could not sleep."

I don't know about you but I like sleep! I like restful, "waking up refreshed" sleep. I like "Good Morning Holy Spirit" sleep.

Did you know that sleep can be a form of worship? It is the ultimate act of trusting God. We all do it; we trust God to sustain us while we sleep. Most nights that is pretty easy to do, but how do you sleep when the worries of this world encamp themselves all around you?

I think about Daniel in the lion's den; it was no surprise to him that he was going into a dangerous situation. He had no control over the outcome. Since Daniel's tendency was to trust God in every situation as a part of his God-centered life, he could continue to pray. For Daniel prayer was both a communion with God and a plea for God's will to be accomplished in his life. Daniel had peace because he believed in the power of his God.

Then there is the **King Darius Sleep Technique**. Upon realizing you are unable to control the outcome, you finally relinquish the situation to God as the last resort. **Verse 18 (ESV)** *reads "Then the king went to his palace and spent the night fasting; no diversions were brought to him, and sleep fled from him."*

Do we delay the manifestation of God's Glory by trying to control desired outcomes in our own power?

Does sleep flee us because we are trying to make sure we get all of the steps right; (fast, pray and mediate), on the word and power of God? We're in such a hurry to receive God's response we still cannot get any rest. **Psalm 127: 2 (NKJV)** *"It is vain for you to rise up early, to sit up late, to eat the bread of sorrows; For so He gives His beloved sleep."*

I pray the **Daniel Sleep Plan** for everyone who chooses to trust in God; to have a living and abiding faith to trust God even in the most difficult circumstances. As for Daniel:

The power of God sent an angel to protect Daniel in response to a prayer of faith coming from a consistent, abiding walk.

Because of this faith, Daniel is recognized in Hebrews 11:33 as one who by faith stopped the mouths of lions.

Nugget of Truth

The next time you can't sleep because of worry or stress, remember that God has a way of working it out if you just rest in Him.

Going to sleep means letting go of our desire to control our world and trusting God to take care of things.

Digging Deeper:

Daniel 6: 1- 23; Psalm 3:5; Psalm 127:2; Hebrews 11:33

— Tracy Dillard

WISDOM NUGGET

Faith in God is the fuel you need to generate miracles.

— Pastor Anthony Turkson

WEEK 33

Don't Prevent the Children from Coming to Jesus

MARK 10:14-15 - NLT

He said to them, "Let the children come to me. Don't stop them! For the Kingdom of God belongs to those who are like these children. I tell you the truth, anyone who doesn't receive the Kingdom of God like a child will never enter it."

I heard a dear mother say "Don't let me stand in the way of any of these young people trying to find you." This should be the collective cry of every adult, an especially the Body of Christ.

I am grieved when I see children being mistreated; those that are missing and exploited. The trauma that this has caused to their spiritual well-being is inexcusable. I often pray that victimized children don't become abusers themselves when they get older.

Mark 9:42 warns that those who cause the little ones who believe and trust in Jesus to stumble [that is to lose faith], it would be better for them to have a millstone put around their neck and drowned.

Psalm 127:3 states that children are a heritage and gift from the Lord.

To you who are parents, teachers, mentors, and coaches, you have future leaders in your charge: doctors, lawyers, scientists, Heads of state, mentors, teachers, and parents.

It is imperative that we don't crush the spirits of our young people. Listen to them. Encourage them. Don't tolerate them but love them and remind them that their lives matter. Because one day when we are old we may find these same children now taking care of us.

Lead them into the Light of God's love. God is watching. What does He see?

— S. Long-Scott

WISDOM NUGGET

If we crush our children's hope we crush our own.

— Stephanie Long-Scott

WEEK 34

Well-Watered Trees

JOB 14:7-9 NKJV

For there is hope for a tree, if it is cut down, that it will sprout again, And that its tender shoots will not cease. Though its root may grow old in the earth, and its stump may die in the ground, yet at the scent of water it will bud and bring forth branches like a plant.

Elders, I am speaking to you. You are survivors. You have survived extreme cold, extreme heat, famine, debt and indebtedness and failure. You have been cast down but not destroyed **(2 Corinthians 4:9)**. You've been cut down by other people's opinions who didn't know who you really were. Why have you survived this long? Because you are a tree of righteousness, the planting of the Lord **(Isaiah 61:3)**.

A tree cannot survive without water. So continue to water your roots with the word daily **(Ephesians 5:26)**.

After all that you've endured, God can still make you like a new plant. He makes everything beautiful in its time **(Ecclesiastes 3:11a)**. It doesn't matter how long you have been planted God is still doing new things so **look ahead** with hope in your heart **(Isaiah 43:18-19, Romans 15:13)**.

God is still able to use you. Thank Him for the chapters in your life that are still being written.

— S. Long-Scott

WISDOM NUGGET

Don't let your expectation be the collective memories of your past.

— Rev. Janice Davis-Steele

WEEK 35

God Will Not Forget You

ISAIAH 49:15-16 - NKJV

Can a woman forget her nursing child, and not have compassion on the son of her womb? Surely they may forget, yet I will not forget you. See, I have inscribed you on the palms of My hands; your walls are continually before Me

---

This indelible mark is a **mark of remembrance**. God knew us before we were formed in our mothers' wombs (**Jeremiah 1:5**).

Jesus offered himself as a sacrificial lamb before the world began proving his pre-existence as God (**Revelation 13:8, 1 Peter 1:18-20**). So this mark signified that Jesus would carry us with him to the cross (**1 Peter 2:24**).

A memorial is a physical structure erected to preserve the memory of someone. The cross of Christ is a living memorial to Jesus (**John 12:32, 1 Corinthians 15:3-4**).

The thief crucified with Christ asked Jesus to **remember** him. Because of God's love the thief entered paradise with the Lord that very day.

Jesus enacted the communion celebration for us to **remember** Him.

Take communion every day this week and reflect on God's love for you. Remember Jesus like He remembers you and fall in love with Him all over again.

— S. Long-Scott

WISDOM NUGGET

We don't go to heaven because we did good. It's because of the good Jesus did. We believe and accept him.

— Pastor Anthony Turkson

WEEK 36

A Preponderance of the Evidence

ROMANS 1:20 – AMP

For ever since the creation of the world His invisible attributes, His eternal power and divine nature, have been clearly seen, being understood through His workmanship [all His creation, the wonderful things that He has made], so that they [who fail to believe and trust in Him] are without excuse and without defense.

I was a juror on a civil case. The case had to be decided on the preponderance of the evidence. This meant that the evidence on one side had to be more convincing than on the other.

I thought about God vs man, evolution, and anything else you may want to put up against Him. In the beginning God ... **(Genesis 1:1)**.

So by a preponderance of the evidence (the universe, earth, moon, sun, fish, animals, plants, people and all living things), God wins. He rests His case **(Psalm 19:1)**.

This week see God's handiwork all around you as if for the first time. Observe the sun and sky. Enjoy a moonlit night; Smell the flowers. Visit water sources and feel the peace of a babbling brook or the waves of the ocean. And know with certainty that **God is.**

— S. Long-Scott

WISDOM NUGGET

For excellence to show the details must not be spared.

— Min. Emmanuel Azu

WEEK 37

Your Family is Large

MATTHEW 19:29

And everyone who has left houses or brothers or sisters or father or mother or wife or children or lands, for My name's sake, shall receive a hundredfold, and inherit eternal life.

You may have come from a dysfunctional family. Your parents may have never said "I love you". You may not have been close to your siblings. You may not have had the emotional support that affected your growth and development.

But here is the good news. If you belong to Christ, you have been adopted into a very large family.

You have brothers and sisters who love you for you. You have mothers and fathers who will advise you just because they love you. You have a host of aunties, uncles, and cousins. Do you see how big your family is now?

Jesus made a significant point about his family in **Matthew 12:48-50** "... Who is My mother and who are My brothers?" And He stretched out His hand toward His disciples and said, "Here are My mother and My brothers! For whoever does the will of My Father in heaven is My brother and sister and mother."

Only God can change the heart of your natural family so roll the care of them over onto God (**1 Peter 5:7**).

Reflect on the spiritual family in whom God has placed you. Embrace them and know that you are not alone. You are loved.

— S. Long-Scott

WISDOM NUGGET

Sometimes we don't see things the way they are.
We see things the way we are.

— Rev. Janice Davis-Steele

WEEK 38

God Speaks To Lions

DANIEL 6: THE LION'S DEN

Reading about Daniel being thrown in the Lion's Den and God shutting the mouth of the lions, reminded me of the story of Balaam in **Numbers 22: 21-35**. God allowed the donkey to see what Balaam could not see; the angel of the Lord standing in the way ready to kill Balaam. Therefore, God used the donkey to save Balaam's life.

In the same way God used the lions to not only spare Daniel's life but also gave him a resting place.

Imagine God having a conversation with the lions: *"Now lions, my son Daniel is going to be thrown in this den with you all. I'm going to need all of you to call a corporate fast while he's here. Not only do I need you to fast, but I also need one of you to sacrifice your body as a pillow for him to rest his head on."*

The lions obeyed the voice of the Lord, and they were blessed and given more than enough food to eat at the end of their fast **(Daniel 6:24)**. Because of Daniel's prayer life and his love for God, God delivered him and made his name great.

I remember the time I was going through with my daughter. We were estranged for a while because of her disobedience and lack of respect for our household. We could not see eye to eye. Those who we had confided in about this betrayed our confidence and became just like the lions that preyed before pouncing (using their tongues to speak against us).

My daughter left home and we had no knowledge of where she was or if she was safe.

During a revival God spoke through our pastor for the ministry team to pray at least 30 minutes before services started asking for the presence of God to move in our midst. One of those nights pastor stated "Whatever is on your heart give it to God and watch Him move on your behalf." So, I started praying about my daughter, just wanting to know that she was safe.

The next day while at work, I received a phone call from my daughter crying and wanting to come home. God answered my prayer speedily. I can only imagine if I had not been obedient to what God called me to do, I would not have received that phone call.

With time and patience God has restored my daughter and my relationship in such a way, you wouldn't know that there was ever an issue between us. God had shut the mouths of the lions.

No matter what happens in your life, when you make up your mind and become obedient to God, He will take care of you. God will prove Himself to you and close the mouth of the lions in your life.

— Deborah Duncan Heard

WISDOM NUGGET

Godly vision overrides evidence.

— REV. JANICE DAVIS-STEELE

WEEK 39

The Past is the Past

2 CORINTHIANS 5:17

Therefore, if anyone is in Christ, he is a new creation; old things have passed away; behold, all things have become new.

This means our past is forgotten and everything ahead of us is new and exciting. God will never bring up our past.

On the other hand, the devil wants us to remember our old life trying to convince us that we haven't changed. He'll send old movie reels of our lives into our minds to keep us from moving forward. But God has given us the ability to take negative thoughts captive **(2 Corinthians 10:5).**

Our minds are not a playground for the devil to come and go as he pleases. **Jeremiah 29:11** says God's thoughts toward us are of peace and not of evil to give us a future and a hope. We must allow God's thoughts to invade our mind through his word.

Keep a journal of the things God has spoken to you. God's word will always point you forward. He has paved a bright and glorious future for you to enjoy. Stay on the path with Him **(Psalm 119:105).**

— S. Long-Scott

WISDOM NUGGET

Don't let the mess stop your press.

— Rev. Janice Davis-Steele

WEEK 40

LIVING WATER

(EZEKIEL 47:1-5)

One of the visions God gave the prophet Ezekiel was of water flowing from under the threshold of the temple. A man went out with a line in his hand, measured the waters and brought Ezekiel through it. The water came to his ankles. The man measured again and the water came to his knees. Again, he measured, and the water came to Ezekiel's waist. Afterward he measured, and it was a river too deep to cross. One would have to swim to cross the river.

As I reflected on Ezekiel's vision, I thought about a time when we All were living in the water of our mother's womb. We were settled, content, and completely dependent on her for sustenance. **Our only mandate was to grow.**

At the appointed time, the water we were living in broke, and suddenly we were released from that warm, and controlled space, into a place that is cooler, eye squinting, and wide open. Birth had taken place. The water we were living in, is Now living in us. **And the mandate to grow continues.** For God has sufficiently supplied us with Grace to Grow in Him.

In time we come to realize that in order to fully grow, we need the help of others: Parents, teachers, ministry leaders, community to help steer us in the right direction. When we discover that the right direction is Jesus and we accept him into our heart, a Rebirth occurs and God Himself begins to parent us.

We are God's temple and the living water of the word of God is in us. It sustains us; Living water flows through the doorway of our temples. As we pour out, it brings life to the lifeless and hope to the hopeless. It helps us grow so we can help others grow. Living water flows through us prompting us to speak the good news of the gospel of Jesus Christ. Good news of salvation and Eternal life; of healing and deliverance; of hope and restoration; of joy and peace. Living water is God himself living in us. The river that will NEVER run dry.

Week Reflection: Remain in the flow of the River. Not only will you live, but also bring life to others.

— Jacqueline Carter

WISDOM NUGGET

We need to change our spiritual perspective.

— Pastor Anthony Turkson

WEEK 41

Beautiful Feet

ISAIAH 52:7 - NKJV

How beautiful upon the mountains are the feet of him who brings good news, Who proclaims peace, Who brings glad tidings of good things, Who proclaims salvation, Who says to Zion, "Your God reigns!"

To God, beautiful feet may not always be the manicured kind. Rather, they are feet that will go wherever God tells them to. These feet are empowered to leave marks in the earth as they triumph over the enemy **(Luke 10:19, Deut. 11:24)**, while taking land for Jesus Christ.

They also know how to stand and maintain their position of faith throughout every trial and testing because these feet are planted on the Rock **(Ephesians 6:10-18)**.

So, how beautiful are your feet?

Think about the impressions your feet have left in the hearts of people. Were they positive or were they negative?

Impressions are not forgotten.

— S. Long-Scott

WISDOM NUGGET

The kingdom of God is not in what you say,
but in what you display.

— Rev. Robin Smiley

WEEK 42

A Love Never Seen Before

JOHN 3:16

"For God so loved the world that he gave his only begotten Son, that whoever believeth in him should not perish, but have everlasting life.

―――― ᵔ ――――

When I think of this scripture God always takes me deeper, because this wasn't just some man on a cross. It was God in the flesh, the Savior of the world Jesus Christ our Lord.

One of the most important things that comes to heart is the Love he demonstrated for us; a love never seen before. God so loved us that he sent His best, Jesus, to reconcile us back to the Father and the unconditional (agape) love he has for us.

This love should now work through us by the power of the Holy Spirit **(Galatians 5:1-2)**. Now as Children of God we humble ourselves to show off this love to others. We are the example of what that love looks like; and yes people should be able to identify the love of God in us.

Sometimes in this cold world you may be the one the Father shines his love through so others will see and glorify him **(John 13:34-35)**. This love we have as born again Children of God should not be taken lightly.

I will be the first to admit you may stumble sometimes. It takes a person that is ready to die to the flesh and submit to the spirit of God **(1 John 2:10)**.

(Agape) love is designed to shape you and build you up to look more like Jesus.

Let's look closely at the cross with Jesus as our example. What do we see?

Take a moment to think about it. Now by the Holy Spirit you should see love, forgiveness of sins, humility, obedience, patience and sacrifice. This was no ordinary love.

Now with the help and leading of the Holy Spirit this love dwells in us and can be expressed through us if we do it his way not ours. This is amazing when you think about it. This is the same love that dwells in you and me.

This love confused the enemy for had he known he would have never crucified our Lord and Savior. Jesus made a show of him openly **(Colossians 2:15)**.

So remember the cross and the love that was expressed for us. Let it be a reminder of how much God loves us and how much he requires us to love others. You can do this.

— Rev. Reginald Johnson

WISDOM NUGGET

Never allow the enemy of your soul to come between you and God who loves you.

— Stephanie Long-Scott

WEEK 43

Tomorrow About This Time

2 KINGS 7:1 - KJV

Then Elisha said, Hear ye the word of the Lord; Thus saith the Lord, To morrow about this time shall a measure of fine flour be sold for a shekel, and two measures of barley for a shekel, in the gate of Samaria.

I experienced this scripture a while ago. I needed a financial windfall at the time and I needed it in 24 Hours. So I decreed that tomorrow about this time I would have the money.

The next morning during prayer, the Lord kept showing me the person to ask. But I kept dismissing the thought. I would have never gone to ask them for anything because I've always seen them struggle in life over the years. But God insisted that I reach out to them. Part of my hesitation was pride because I didn't want to appear that I couldn't handle my business.

I finally got over myself and called. I was glad the answering machine came on because I wasn't ready for a voice to voice conversation. So I left a message. 2 hours later I got a call telling me that I could come and pick up the money. Exactly 24 Hours from the time I made my decree I had a check in my hand.

With God ALL things are possible **(Matthew 19:26)**. What He did for me He will certainly do for you. Faith is an action word. This week be strengthened and encouraged to believe God beyond what you see.

— S. Long-Scott

WISDOM NUGGET

Believing God will cost you unbelief.

— Min Emmanuel Azu

WEEK 44

Beware of the Company You Keep

1 CORINTHIANS 15:33 - KJV

Be not deceived: evil communications corrupt good manners.

PROVERBS 13:20 - NLT

Walk with the wise and become wise; associate with fools and get in trouble.

Judas walked with Righteousness but still committed an unrighteous act of betrayal. He left his company of believers, his covering, for the lust of money. **John 12:6** states that Judas was the treasurer and a thief. This was the door he left open for the devil to enter and use him.

Didn't Judas witness the miracles that Jesus performed? Didn't he go out and evangelize? But his heart was far from Jesus **(Matthew 15:8)**.

Though the Bible prophesied that Jesus would be betrayed, it didn't have to be Judas. When Judas realized the gravity of his sin it was too late. He had ostracized himself from Jesus. The Scribes and Pharisees who used Judas didn't want to have anything to do with him either.

We have to walk circumspectly in this life because our adversary is looking for an entry point into our lives to lure us away from God **(1 Peter 5:8)**.

This week assess the company that you keep. Some changes may be necessary.

— S. Long-Scott

WISDOM NUGGET

I am worthy in His identity.

— Min. Tracy Dillard

WEEK 45

Cut the Umbilical Cord

It's hard to let go of our children as they approach adulthood. We have a storehouse of memories of when they were born, the first steps they took, the first word they spoke, etc. We spend our lives dedicated to taking care of them hoping to leave a legacy of remembrance to the generations that follow.

I got mad at God once during a discussion about my son. He allowed me to argue with Him **(Isaiah 43:26)**. I pleaded my case, citing the responsibilities that came with raising a son. Then God told me that my son was His son first. You would think that would be enough to calm me down but I kept going.

The next morning I came to myself and fell to my knees in repentance. I was grateful that God had allowed me to live as I slept for the disrespectful way that I spoke to Him. I felt God's peace all around me and knew that I had been forgiven.

It wasn't long after that during prayer I had a vision of my son and I attached to an umbilical cord. God said it was time to cut it. He said that it would be painful but that we would be alright. I saw the giant pair of scissors separating us. And yes it was painful but God made it well with my son and me.

Who needs to cut the cord and entrust their children to God's care? If you don't your children will be morally, emotionally, and spiritually handicapped. If you've trained them as God has led you then they are going to be okay **(Proverbs 22:6)**.

— S. Long-Scott

WISDOM NUGGET

Vision with no purpose is blurred.

— Rev. Janice Davis Steele

WEEK 46

Break Through to Your Breakthrough

MICAH 2:13 – AMPC

The Breaker [the Messiah] will go up before them. They will break through, pass in through the gate and go out through it, and their King will pass on before them, the Lord at their head.

Breakthrough: An instance of achieving success in a particular sphere or activity; discovery

Break Through: To force your way through something that's stopping you from moving forward

Whatever is blocking our blessings must be moved out of the way. We have to **break through** to discover what God has already prepared for us. **Philippians 3:13-14 (AMP)** says it best: *Brothers and sisters, I do not consider that I have made it on my own yet; but one thing I do: forgetting what lies behind and reaching forward to what lies ahead, I press on toward the goal to win the [heavenly] prize of the upward call of God in Christ Jesus.*

So don't look back unless you are measuring how far you have come. His grace is sufficient enough to get us over and around any barrier. **2 Samuel 22:30/Psalm 18:29** both state: For by You I can run against a troop; by my God I can leap over a wall.

The Word which we speak is the weapon we use. But you must believe what you say (**2 Corinthians 4:13**).

The joy of the Lord is the **strength** we use to propel us forward (**Nehemiah 8:10**).

This week let God show you how to apply the pressure, using the appropriate scriptures, in order to achieve your **breakthrough**. Stay on the offensive using those very scriptures and watch the devil run away from you. Why? Because the Lord Jesus himself has already prepared the way for you.

— S. Long-Scott

WISDOM NUGGET

Don't be stuck in a place that has no part in your future.

— Rev. Janice Davis-Steele

WEEK 47

Unsung Heroes

Unsung Defined – Not celebrated or praised; unacknowledged

God creates encounters that can change the course of destiny for all the people involved. We're all candidates for doing great things for God. Even if we're not well-known on earth, we are known in heaven when we walk in righteousness with God!

The following are accounts of people recorded in the Bible whose names we don't know. God saw fit to acknowledge them because of the vital impact their lives had on others:

2 Kings 5:1-19 – Naaman was healed of leprosy through the influence of **a servant girl** who his army had captured from Israel. This young girl waited on Naaman's wife. She pleaded with her mistress to tell Naaman to seek the prophet Elisha who was in Samaria who would heal him. So Naaman went to Elisha. Upon obeying Elisha's instructions Naaman was finally healed which caused him to turn his heart to the Lord.

2 Samuel 20:1-2, 16-22 – This is the story of Sheba who incited a rebellion against King David. Joab the captain of David's army went in pursuit of Sheba. They found him in Abel of Beth Maachah and began to batter the wall of the city in order to get in and seize Sheba. But **a wise woman** cried out for her city and prevented Joab from destroying it. She reasoned with Joab, promising that Sheba's head would be delivered to him…and it was. Satisfied, Joab departed with this woman's city unharmed and intact.

John 6:1-15 – 5,000 men (not including the women and children) were fed with **a little boy's lunch**. He had five loaves and two fish which the Lord Jesus blessed and multiplied. The Bible doesn't say whether the boy offered his food or was asked, but everyone knows this Bible story whether you're a believer or not. Though **this little boy's mother is not mentioned**, she is probably the one who prepared his meal.

Luke 23 – The thief on the cross who became a evangelist. Those that witnessed the crucifixion of Jesus heard this man defending the Lord. Afterwards the thief turned to Jesus and asked him to remember him. This was the moment of the thief's repentance as his heart turned towards God for salvation.

The thief teaches us all that in the last moments of your life you can give your life to Jesus. He teaches us that it doesn't matter how you start in life but how you finish. This account shows that God resist the proud but extends his grace to the humble, in this case, saving grace **(1 Peter 5:5)**.

God knows who you are. **Psalm 139: 16-17 (NLT)** – *You saw me before I was born. Every day of my life was recorded in your book. Every moment was laid out before a single day had passed. How precious are your thoughts about me, O God.*

Reflect on this: **God will make your name great** and you will have impact.

— S. Long-Scott

WISDOM NUGGET

Don't try to be somebody else; it's already taken.

— Pastor Anthony Turkson

WEEK 48

Work With God to Get God Results

2 CORINTHIANS 6:1 - TPT

Now, since we are God's coworkers, we beg you not to take God's marvelous grace for granted, allowing it to have no effect on your lives.

Do you realize that after you've prayed to God for something, he involves you in bringing the answer? No prayer comes to fruition without our participation. God isn't going to allow us to fold our arms while he does all the work.

I recently saw how I had to work with God to see the results of an issue I had placed before him. It required written documents, phone calls, gifts, and words of encouragement given by me to someone. God was telling me what to do and how to do it. This person was difficult but God's grace was sufficient.

While God worked on their heart he worked on mine. The result was that God was glorified and I rejoiced.

The moral here is don't be the hindrance to your prayers being answered.

Philippians 2:13 says for it is God working through us both to will and to do of His good pleasure.

Reflect on where you may have closed your heart to God. How did your attitude prevent God from accomplishing His purpose in your life? Then repent, yield, and let God have his way.

— S. Long-Scott

WISDOM NUGGET

The living spirit of faith drawing upon the living Word of God to produce living results.

— Rev. Janice Davis-Steele

WEEK 49

I Know, But!

But defined: an argument against something; an objection

"But" negates everything said prior to it.

God knows we're going to ask questions about our lives. In **Isaiah 43:26** God tells us to put him in remembrance; pleading our case before him in order to vindicate ourselves. So He welcomes dialogue.

However, when God puts his foot down on an issue, that's when all questioning must end. Then it's on us to come into agreement with the one that has the final say **(Amos 3:3)**.

No more "I know, but".

His word is a lamp unto our feet (to see our feet) and a light unto our pathway (in order to see where God is taking us) **(Psalm 119:105)**.

When God gives command, a simple "Yes Lord" is sufficient.

Reflect on **Ecclesiastes 12:13**: *Let us hear the conclusion of the matter: Fear God and keep his commandments: for this is the whole duty of man.*

— S. Long-Scott

WISDOM NUGGET

What God has called us to do is not subject to change.

— Stephanie Long-Scott

WEEK 50

From Thief to Evangelist

I was reflecting on the penitent thief crucified along with Jesus in **Luke 23:39-43**. He lived a life of stealing from others and was facing his end. I asked Holy Spirit what was the thief's divine purpose since he lived a life of crime. He said **evangelist**. I said "What?" Then Holy Spirit explained.

The people gathered at Calvary could hear the conversation the thief was having with Jesus. He first spoke to the other condemned thief about Jesus' innocence. He's dying on the cross yet testifying to the goodness of Jesus.

Then he turned to Jesus and said *"Remember me"*. And Jesus responded: *"Assuredly, I say to you, today you will be with Me in Paradise."* A life of thievery turned around in a moment. He received the plan of salvation in two words: **"Remember me"**.

Here is the lovingkindness and tender mercies of God on display. I imagined some of those watching and listening to the thief's exchange with Jesus had a change of heart and repented. **Ecclesiastes 7:8a** says "Better is the end of a thing than the beginning thereof."

It doesn't matter your status in life, or how you began; God will help you to fulfill your purpose.

If you are not sure, ask God what your purpose in life is. Write down what He says. He knows you better than you know yourself.

— S. Long-Scott

WISDOM NUGGET

The kingdom of God is something to receive not achieve.

— Tracy Dilliard

WEEK 51

O King, Live Forever!

In the book of Daniel, we see this statement five times "O king, live forever". Initially, when reading it we can deduce that it's a salutation to the king. However, as we study the verses prior to the statement, each time we see that it is made after a time of distress, or anxiety, either that of the king or those making the statement.

There will be times in our lives where we may find ourselves distressed, anxious, or even afraid. Our natural response to those emotions should be "O king, live forever!" You may be saying to yourself, why should this be my response? Well, here's why.

First, God promised that He is a very present help in our time of need (**Psalm 46:1, Hebrews 4:16**). So crying out "O king, live forever", reminds our soul (our mind, will, emotions, intellect, and imagination) that *"greater is He that is in me, than he that is in the world"* (**1 John 4:4**).

Second, **Philippians 4:6** commands us to bring our anxiety, fears, and feelings of distress to God. When we do, we are guaranteed to receive the peace of God that surpasses all understanding.

Third, we should say "O king, live forever" to ourselves or to those that may find themselves dealing with these emotions, because **1 Peter 2:9** tells us that we are royalty. **Revelation 5:10** reminds us that we have been made kings and priests. Therefore, we must see ourselves the way God sees us. And when the enemy tries to bring on the spirit of anxiety, depression, defeat, etc., our spirit man must arise and say, "O king live forever!"

A time of reflection:

1. What areas of your life do you need to say "O king, live forever"? Write them down and ask the Holy Spirit to show you how to surrender them to Him.

2. Who do you know that needs to be reminded to say "O king, live forever"? Write the names down and make a point to contact them before the end of the week.

— Rev. Robin Smiley

WISDOM NUGGET

Allow God to introduce you to YOU.

— Stephanie Long-Scott

WEEK 52

Love Forgave Us All

LUKE 23:33-34 NKJV

And when they had come to the pace called Calvary, there they crucified Him, and the criminals, one on the right hand and the other on the left. Then Jesus said, "Father, forgive them for they do not know what they do."

How great is God's love that at the point of death Jesus was still on the mission of saving souls. There were two criminals dying with Jesus but only one believed in his sacrifice for sin. And that thief became a saint. Glory to God!

You, who like the thief, thought that his life would end tragically without God, can come to Jesus right now and let him become your Savior and Lord. Invite Jesus into your heart. It's a spiritual transaction, a covenant that you are entering in with God through the shed blood of His son Jesus.

We who are already saints of the Most High God welcome you to the family.

To all the Saints the work of salvation continues according to the Apostle Paul in **Hebrews10**: Verse 22, "**Let us** draw near (to God) in full assurance of faith; Verse 23, "**Let us** hold fast (grip) the confession of our hope without wavering; Verse 24, "**Let us** consider one another to stir up love and good works. **Hebrews 12:1**, "**Let us** lay aside every weight and sin that so easily besets us and **let us** run with patience (endurance) the race that is set before us.

Let us live an abundant life with Christ.

— S. Long-Scott

WISDOM NUGGET

Stop fighting God. Allow Him to process you.

— STEPHANIE LONG-SCOTT

A Culmination of these 52 Weeks:

Encountering God through the Sowing of His Word (The Seed)

Encounters Defined: Unexpected experiences or an unexpected meeting with someone or something.

You have encountered God during these 52 weeks of devotionals. He's been depositing seed into your heart without you realizing it. Actually God's been dropping seed onto the soil of your heart all your life. He has been involved in the planting, the watering and the increase of the fruit produced in you. You've heard God's voice even when you didn't know it was Him speaking. If you've ever said "Something told me," and it was good advice, chances are that was God speaking to you.

Matthew 13 tells us that God Himself is the Sower of His Word. His word has so much power in itself to impact your life on purpose **(Isaiah 55:10-11)**.

God's word entering our hearts is dependent upon several factors:

Understanding - When we don't understand what God is saying the seed of His word isn't able to penetrate our heart and take root. We must ask God to help us understand **(Isaiah 11:3, Psalm 111:10, 2 Timothy 2:7)**.

Knowing God - To know God is to trust God. To trust God is to obey God. Trust causes humility which allows God's seed to enter your heart **(Philippians 3:7-10)**.

An Open heart - An open heart is a tender heart. Our hearts have to be primed to receive seed. This is the tenderizing process **(Ezekiel 36:26)** done by the hand of God.

Loving God – One of the greatest commandments is to love God. **Mark 12:30** tells us that we are to love the Lord our God with all our heart, and with all our soul, and with all our mind, and with all our strength. This means every aspect of our lives is involved in loving God; our gifts, talents, resources, and time.

Change how you think - Don't allow your own understanding to reject the move of God in your life **(Proverbs 3:5-6)**. Get God's perspective and you won't fail. Do things God's way and you will get God results.

Finally, know that YOU are a seed planted by God in the earth. He predetermined when you would be born, where you would live, what you would look like and do. He imparted gifts and talents inside of you. He watered you and pruned you so that you would flourish and bear fruit **(Acts 17:26-28)**.

You have encountered yourself as you have read this devotional. There will be more to encounter and receive from God as you become aware of His presence. Go back and travel through this devotional again and again.

A Prayer of Thanksgiving

What can I say unto the Lord? All I have to say is "Thank you Lord!" Thank you Lord! Thank you Lord! Thank you for the breath in my body. Thank you for a sound mind. Thank you for a voice that can praise you and shout "Hallelujah Jesus!" Thank you for ears to hear and eyes to see. Thank you for the daily bread you always provide. Thank you for loving me and sending Jesus to save me. Thank you for filling me with your precious Spirit. Thank you for my prayer language. Thank you for your continued mercy and faithfulness. If I had 10,000 tongues it still wouldn't be sufficient to tell you how grateful I am. Thank you for counting me as a vessel that you can use. It is a privilege and an honor to serve you.

WISDOM NUGGET

Human should also stand for 'humble man' when we reflect on how great and mighty God is.

— STEPHANIE LONG-SCOTT

The Road to Hell

The road to hell is a paved superhighway full of twists and turns and detours leading the Unsuspected away from the road to heaven.

Street names like **Deception** and **Alternative** avenues, along with **Enticing Bridge** makes it difficult to discern which road to take.

This serves only to complicate ones decision to get on the **Right Road** to salvation. **Right Road** will lead you to **Come To Yourself Junction** where, when you look up ahead, you'll see the **Way Truth and Life Street**. This street is narrow and at times, not even paved. But there is a constant **Light** glowing ahead even in the dark giving you a direct route to heaven.

Once on it, **Right Road** will begin to seem familiar to you; for it leads you back to your origins from whence you came, heaven.

Matthew 7:13-14 (KJV)

[13] Enter ye in at the strait gate: for wide is the gate, and broad is the way, that leadeth to destruction, and many there be which go in thereat:

[14] Because strait is the gate, and narrow is the way, which leadeth unto life, and few there be that find it.

John 14:6 (KJV)

[6] Jesus saith unto him, I am the way, the truth, and the life: no man cometh unto the Father, but by me.

The Prayer of Salvation

If you have never confessed Jesus as Lord of your life according to **Romans 10:9-10**, then please say the following prayer:

Lord Jesus,

I know that I am a sinner, and I ask for your forgiveness. I believe you died for my sins and rose from the dead. Come into my heart and take over my life. I receive you as Lord and Savior. Thank you for cleansing me of my sins and making me new in my spirit again.

If you have prayed this prayer, welcome to the family of God. The Holy Spirit is now residing in your reborn human spirit. He will guide you to find a Bible-believing church where the word of God is taught and applied. The Bible is your road map for life. It will never lead you astray as you allow Holy Spirit to guide you.

"The Lord bless you and keep you; The Lord make His face shine upon you, and be gracious to you; The Lord lift up His countenance upon you, and give you peace." **(Numbers 6:24-26)**

— S. Long-Scott

Made in the USA
Columbia, SC
10 April 2025